EMBLEMS

OF

PASSAGE

Jeannette

Nichols

RUTGERS UNIVERSITY PRESS · New Brunswick, New Jersey

Grateful acknowledgment is made to the following publications for permission to reprint poems which originally appeared in them:

American Weave: Dachau and After; Frank O'Hara and Ignoble Death; Stones.
The Atlantic Monthly: Birthday in the House of the Poor.
Harper's Magazine: Bicycle.
Massachusetts Review: It Will Happen.
Prairie Schooner: One Woman's Words.
Saturday Review: Halfway; Hidden in Hair; Imaginary Companion; Magic-Box Maker; My Son, Momentum; Poem for David 8 & Open; Something About to Happen; The Last One In; The Moment; The Road; To My Nephew Headed Everywhere; Wind in the Wells.
Southern Review: House.
Yale Literary Magazine: Thirty-Nine Sounds for Soft Singing.
Yankee: The Smallest of Things; Twilight, Not Now.

". . . scapegoats, husks, emblems of passage;
a passage not easy, not now, not here, not
to be apprehended except when it is
unattainable . . ."

from *A Passage to India*
by E. M. Forster

for
my Mother, my Father . . .
emblems of strength, of sensitivity. . . .

CONTENTS

Part I

Part II

Part III

PART I

SOMETHING ABOUT TO HAPPEN

[for Uta Hagen and Herbert Berghof]

Something is about to happen.
Something is always about to happen.

I acquire the grace to move toward you.
You are about to happen. To me.

I learn your name. We slowly
get older making up names for our acts.

If I am going to love you
I am always going to love you.

We die and
we are always going to die.

Acquiring the grace
is more difficult than loving.

TO MY NEPHEW HEADED
EVERYWHERE

There are roads
but some find the sky easiest
and steps and tunnels

if you grow tired leaping
cut notches in the wind
try sleeping sideways

avoid drinking the water anywhere
melons, peaches, slow-lapped dew from grass blades
will do the same job

bring only what you can wear
carry no worries
wet your finger and hold it up for which way love
        comes.

I'll not be there
nor will you remember me
nor anyone near you now learning to save ourselves
        only.

There are roads
and islands of air
and no one here or there can guarantee light passage.

Wave from the window
of your life
goodbye, goodbye.

BIRTHDAY IN THE HOUSE
OF THE POOR

This is the house
of the poor.
        Today
I am come to 90 years
like a doorstep.
          There is
no hope on the hall table.
          The State
is my father, my mother
is the cook here
and never gives me enough.
          When are you
coming, I mean I couldn't bear
to see you even then
              but when?
This is my room in this house
of the poor, and this
is my window.
          I own all outside it
as far as the peach tree which
no longer bears. We are
sisters.
    . When you don't come
I will write again, when you don't write
I will say the $2 you didn't send
got lost.
          But please write,

send money, and come
                    though I don't
want you to see me here, though
this poor house could never be home
even if I had money
                    or even if you'd come.

POEM FOR DAVID
8 & OPEN

He was 8
and brought in an armful
of hard tar.

Later, brought
it in again
cubed in a tub of water.

Asked why
he said *to see*
what it's made of.

Tar is made
of tar
I nearly said

before I saw the man
walk out of the boy
with an armful of tar

an armful
of what
everything's made of.

THE WOMAN IN THE MOTOR CHAIR

The woman
in the motor chair
goes home
alongside cars
faithfully safe.

Even
in the rain
her solid small chair
hums home under streetlights,
over streetslick.

Sometimes
she waves if it's April
and the wind's soft,
sometimes
she stops and talks
if it's early
and someone smiles.

She's with us
all our lives
seated and hardly ever older.

She goes by
in the most amazing
of weathers
wishing us if not well
at least even chances.

Wherever she goes it takes her longer.

ONE WOMAN'S WORDS

I am becoming round
and reaching,
find.
    Kiss
and good night.

Round I am getting
and all smiles.
Whispers follow me
like smoke,
        like kisses.
Ah, good night, good night.

TWO WEEKS GOODBYE

[for James Richard Banks 1910–1965]

Today is two weeks goodbye
and birds like flags
gather in first snow singing
of hungers and hello.

You are nowhere we know of
yet we arrive there
in love with all your names.

Another life begins
like a movie
to your scenario

and we go forward
with your permissions
like tickets.

Although today is two weeks
goodbye and the ice of the world
is a warning,
                        we breathe
on our hands now
as you
on our hearts
have.

DYING AS GIFT

[for Millicent 1931–1959]

bonum per accidens, ex casu

*"Life is sometimes good, and death is
sometimes good. Life is no more a good
in itself than any other value is. It is good,
when and if it is good, because of the
context. When it is not good, it deserves
neither protection nor preservation."*

Joseph Fletcher

I have lived for this
though not enough

Mother, give me the pills!

What's left
of my seed-pod body
is set adrift
beneath these sheets

mother, mother . . .

the pills are a boat
I've sailed from pain, mother,
I'll sail away again . . .

Why hold me here
till even my body turns black

mother, mother, the pills . . .

I've no more knack
for life than god has.

GIVE ME BACK WHAT YOU GAVE.

I wave from this boat of pain
and won't come back
though the air is thick as the sea

though I can't see you
and you *won't* see me

give me the pills, mother,
the ticket, the price, mother,

to die, to go
and never come back

mother, mother . . .

PARADE

He has no horn, nor drum,
nor any small flag.

The poor have their whistles.

Only that inner instrument
has he, a uniform of smiles
and the wish to march.

The hungry have their legs.

He awakens
a surprise of hands at the ends of his arms
to begin again
the new music.

The loved are sleeping out his dawn.

He begins. A parade
of one
still a parade.

LUCKING OUT

Home
from the flight
we've lucked out again

the wheel spins and it's not our number.

The windows are the same
but look out differently or in
on our difference

death was saying another name

and we're here
laying out food, pouring out
milk, sitting down
to the good meal.

The clover with its extra leaf
dries in our book
sleeps with its dry face
against a good word

death somewhere
is calling out numbers

and it is not yet time.

THE MOMENT

We *find out*
and Betrayal
moves into the next room

the moment stands in wet shoes

and we go after
asking and wringing
our hands

Betrayal stands
in the doorway
a silhouette in cut paper

and we *walk out*

the moment turns and turns
then goes out
like a damp candle.

THE LAST ONE IN

O the last one in
cried because everything
was eaten

and sat down and beat
his head on the floor
calling all who came before

unfair. All we could do
was go out single file
like snuffed candles

leaving our smoke
and the dishes. But O the last was
first up the next day

and ate enough for two.
So it goes. Even the wronged
go wrong.

A CHINESE POET DANCES EXERCISES:

A crane
rises
from the water

the dragon
is pushed back

the monkey
turns over and
over

frees
the dancer
to pivot

on one foot

to stand
for one moment
like a stork

then move
wrist on wrist
enclosing

the animal
he is

a bird
whose song
ripples the surface

of silence:

water
of darkness
he dances in.

FEET

Laid out
the toenails
keep growing.
Now
they are going
nowhere, sleep
is their motion.
They point
in, big toe
touching big toe
like praying
from the wrong
end. They
could be going
downtown, but
here they are
dreaming
of walking
in rivers of love
pedi-
cured of
loss and
empty travel.

THE ROAD

It goes. Eliding
over the hilltop
and doesn't stop anywhere,
goes into its brother
as if it owed a debt.

It comes back
like a lover from another
woman, reeking of lives
and the deaths of small animals.

It is. As a life
is, complete unto itself
only after we
the living
have entered into it
like a death
going everywhere.

FRANK O'HARA AND
IGNOBLE DEATH

Something absurd
beach buggy out of the tourist world
all glisten and summer passage from beach to beach,
something undeniable did you in
so your life lurched
and fell over like a dead chair.
                                    But
there's Pollock and Schwartz, all the others.
Shake hands with Camus, Frank, have the good laugh
                                    on us all.

BE KINDER
[for D. L.]

Be kinder. I held
your head and said
You are not as alone as you think,
none of us are.
              You slept when we left,
slept as if we'd never brought you home,
never filled your alone with our own sadness.

Be kinder. I don't mind how you
enter rooms now, nor call across faces of friends.
I know kindness leaps in your roots like April
though you talk at the top of your voice
to the world at large in a room,
address those gods of your life
hoping for friends.
              Oh, be kinder,
to that boy in your chest, man in your loins,
child in your heart. That braggart in your head
is kind, is sweet though alone
as all of us are who do not come
to hold a friend's head and
whisper our own wishes in his ear.

BEACHED WHALE

There's no hope for him.
Hawsers won't reach
he's up too far
and wheezes there
poor old geezer.
.In houses
nearby
they hear him breathe last breaths
and sigh when he's done
turning from his dark hulk
toward tasteless meals.
They think,
nights when all shadows
are humps,
We're all done for
like that
reaching too far
dry-beached and breathing
our last best breaths,
while the whales
deep and down under
sleeping in blubber lumps
dream those inner reaches
of held breath and the rest
in which
hope
has no part.

WIND IN THE WELLS

The wells are chewing
their dark water
and the wind
is asking
to be let in

at last having learned to fear the dark

and in the dried grasses
rodents bring whispers
in from the fields
to hide in our cellars.

Only the moon knows its loneliness
and does what it can
in spite of it

while mud-ruts in the road
harden like worry
and frost bleeds into the ground.

Just at midnight
the moon looks into each well separately,
hesitates like cream

married to the dark beneath,

and the wind is a woman
moving on to other
entrances.

PART II

PART II

TWILIGHT, NOT NOW

It was someone else,
somewhere else
in some other time.

The sidewalk
wore a chalked Miro
where a name
ran into the moon
and outlines
of hands
reached into grass.

Twilight,
the sound of dishes,
groan of porch steps and a screen door
slammed.
In a blink
street lights coming on,
beginning of shadows
and no way out
for someone standing
at the edge of anywhere
calling

where are you?

to someone else,
somewhere else
in some other time.

HALFWAY

We lived
on a hill
halfway

so
it was
up to school
and down to swim

gravity
the friend
of choice.

Winters
we went up
to come down
all the way

sliding
by home
as if it were
a port

and summers
we bicycled down
no-hands

turning our bodies
like wands
before we hit the sea.

We lived
halfway between
growing up
and calming down

there
on a hill
amid heats of disaster
and chills of dare

halfway here
halfway there.

BICYCLE

Spokes all
one moving gleam

the shine
the pure line of going

to lean
make the corner clean

while the sun melts
on the chrome a moving mercury

the whish of wheel on tar
and the going

the holding on
a power of knowing

how fast *fast* is
as the hill hisses past

and the tar slurs
to a soft rubber stop

only to start up again
the going, the greased ease

of red-chrome three-gear
going, going, going. . . .

ANYTHING AT ALL

O you could
draw anything
given the right wall

anything at all
could leap down from your making
for whoever believed

what your hands
made happen—
anything at all.

O you'd come calling
under our windows
while the moon licked December's bones
and we'd run
falling over ourselves

to watch you draw angels
in the new snow

and flailing your arms you'd laugh
at anything at all

and anything at all
was true

when O we loved you.

MAGIC-BOX MAKER

The magic-box maker
is mad
some say

in his box of herbs
he grows words
of a music unblemished
by sense

logic quirks in his head
a world
of mirrors and
nothing is that is

though all will be
as he makes
his mind's magic.

Though some say
he was born mad
and dies madder

I say
he lived
in my head's house
one day

and I too
am as joyfully mad
as the magic-box maker

as mad
as some say
who know only sense

the word without music.

HOUSE

I'm in a white garden. Just arrived.
From a long journey. My luggage
waits on the steps outside the gate.
Beside the pool are white flowers fragrant
with pasts, lazy as broken statues.
No one meets me. I walk, humming.
Why this garden should be white
is no mystery.
            I have arrived
with all the facts. With luggage.

And there the house, lazy, waiting, rooms
like mouths without teeth, smiles without lips
where a doll with broken arms
rides the years out in her windowsill
and bats hang in closets like leather purses.

It is this
white house I have returned to, no other, this
white garden my first arrival.
                 Where I walk
the stagnant pool holds goldfish big as fists,
tarnished, aged white and old as I am.
They keep their secrets, I keep mine.

I walk, place a bench upright,
glance again at the house, again at the garden
(am I just returned?) in which
I am turned path by path toward that
hulk, huge in its white body,
Moby of a house,
depot of departures
where
I
  finally
am come.

IMAGINARY COMPANION

She has spilled the water
and *She* is running
away and away is where
She is safe and light as sea-spray.

She makes each day's plans
using my hands
to play them out.
She she says is never
going to die and
She never cries.

I go with her, talk
with her, reason with her.
She owns everything,
wins everything, is going
to get everything.

Only one day *She* is pale
as lilac wind, and laughs
softer than the sound
of the water
I find myself
spilling.

HOLY COMMUNION

Lay out the lettuce
I shall lie down on it

with the blood of holy tomatoes

and the kindness
deep in me like seeds.

The refrigerator is too cold
and I am not dying

I who am pale as the core
of a radish.

All day all night
the light stays on

without sleep I bless icecubes

believing the vegetables
will rise in their bright skins

scrubbed sinless, body and blood.

MY SON, MOMENTUM

Always it is night
and the world is moving away
wheel in a wheel

my son, Momentum, goes after.

All night
the light stays on
keeping sleep's caution
and the door latch lit.

My daughter, Distraction,
comes in late
singing of fresh loves

the light has never been for her.

I hang up my rings
in the hooks of light,
hang up shadows
of my fingers

while the wheel turns
and time turns me
into what
I am become

more self than most
less lost

as the world moves away
and my son
because he must

goes after.

MYTH: FOR CAMUS

I

The Absurd. Ha and hello.
In a telephone booth
the phone rings
beside a gas station
where a banner billows
                            CLOSED.

II

Hello to you, Suicide. Say, now
that life is home
how was the money spent?
You hoarded it, remember, against
the rainy hope of travel
only to spend it on
                    this death
                    costing nothing.

III

Now, Mr. Absurd, I just got home myself.
How could I know our house
was burning down,
                        and how come
your eyes are the color of smoke?

IV

Mrs. Dolly took you on and O her legs
laid out easy. Enter laughing, Death.

V

Dear Sir, I've opted out, not quite
perfect, but all wrong
loving this tree I'm wrapt around.

I hear a telephone ring
in and out of G of A of S
and all the voices
                    are CLOSED.

HALF-LIGHT

I meet you
in half-light.

I ask
for whom are you looking,
for what?

You say
there is a house
you are searching,
a room,
a chair.

It's this half-light
I tell you,
we all grow lost.

There is a chair
I am thinking of,
one I have worn smooth.
I think to offer it,
my room,
my house.

Then I remember
you'd lose your way
even there
though I took your hand,

though I pushed you gently
into the chair, that chair
worn to the curves
of a woman.

I offer you only
the half-light
as I have owned it
and as I too
am lost in it.

LOVING

If we give it
we give everything it is, it's colors
like falling glass in a tube,
it's motion as lyric
as a stand of bending trees
loving lost breezes. It gives itself
as we have taught it, child of our longing.

It is shape and changing shape
all tree's fruit and the weather
of that change. Wind-bells enter it
and go off from it carillon carillon
Bach for tree-harpsichord or water lute.

We learn
never to reach for it, never
to name it, never to expect it from the next lips.

It lives
in the street of no numbers
and can't be summoned.

We give it
not to be called back.

NEVER THE SAME

It's never the same.
I hold your life in my hands.
You hold mine.
            Without thinking even
we apply pressure. There are more ways
than one to bleed. How carefully
we both hold need's sugar cube
on our tongues, even our saliva
with a life of its own.
            Never the same
you smooth my life over your hand
like a glove.
            I hold yours
like a bird breathing.

GOODBYE TO THAT

We rarely agree
but goodbye
to that
     and
we like what
neither of us is
and
      goodbye to that.
Meeting again
when our minds walk
out on our lives
we'll smile
and say
      well
goodbye to that too.
It's been
      and hello
      to that.

STONES

All day
we gather stones
for the cairns.

Gulls coast close
thinking our hands
hold living crumbs.

We hold aloft a speech of stones,
a gesture, lonely utterance,

crumbs to feed these dead.

The dying lie down laughing
at the absurdity of lilies
held in their hands.

We gather more stones, more gulls.

It gets dark
and the dying do what they do best, talented
hands crossed, eyes testing sleep.

We keep it up all night
and the cairns grow magnificent
until dawn

when we walk away
rehearsing our talent.

DACHAU AND AFTER

I walked out of Dachau
waving my tattoo

yet I have never been there

wept at what I sold
to buy my life

yet never asked the price

held my heart in my hands
like loathesome meat

and could not eat.

I have walked out
stigmata on my hands

and never owned the pain

walked out
to enter this inhuman rain of hate

and sit once more before a plate of love.

THE SMALLEST OF THINGS

Violets, lilies of the valley, forget-me-nots,
the smallest of things
in their time, transcendental air
in mornings when no one
is using the world, each
in its month
owning time as no one else
dares own it,
being
only and smallest and almost
unbelievable, and of anyone's uses
the most possible,
joy the vehicle
of being
only.

PART III

IT WILL HAPPEN

There will be the middle suddenly
like walking into a conversation.
You will go on from there.
                          It will happen
in a meadow of silken grass, and it will
begin like startled birds and form
as collective flight is formed. You will
speak and be part of it
all the way to the end
when the birds settle back
as quietly as blown pollen.
                          The sunlight
will have been stolen and put back,
the order undisturbed. You will
walk away leaving only a form
of flat grass beginning to spring
back from its woman shape.

ALL NIGHT

All night
you sleep with me.
It was something else
I wanted.
These fugitive bells
take me
as daylight takes us both.
What I wanted
was the hush before
these bells awoke.
We sleep,
are taken unaware
and morning
opens its hours
like arms.

CITY OF STRANGERS

That day
I said *I do not belong to you*
I was come to the City of Strangers without luggage
where no one lets you in
without at least one valise
to show you own your life.
And I told them I was someone's wife (not
wanting to use your name) but still
no room. I showed them my paper bag of sandwiches
and the tickets punched for a husband's bed
and still they withheld their rooms of sleep.
So I kept on looking until now
and I am here, pocket full of used tickets,
an empty paper bag and no sleep.
Please forgive what I said
while I was gone
and take me in.
Tell me I belong, lie down
with me. My name to last a life
is Wife.

WHAT LOVE IS

From my mouth
to your mouth
a mouthful of tea.
The hot. The surprise.
The melting
intimacy.

Today
I could think of
no better gift.

As if
I could pour into you
what love is.

MAN/HUSBAND

The beauty
of your buttocks
your back
wounds me

the knife of your turning away
turns me to this

how your thighs slip down
slim as a boy's
soft backs of your knees

kisses alive in your parts like winds

turned
you are without knowledge
until
my cupped palm
touches your buttock curve
as it would the cheek of a boy.

HIDDEN IN HAIR

Something
to take it down
and wear it like any Godiva

you my good horse

to part it
and let the breasts point
slightly down

good to find this hostel
to flesh

of deep brown
and good
to hide in

then to dress it up fresh
as ladies do

and laugh
because nothing of this
is true

my good horse

THIRTY-NINE SOUNDS
FOR SOFT SINGING

Kiss toe knee
  and
     and
       and
  me my lips
  till I twirl my heels
  dip down the dark
  fall up the light
  and roll round the corner dew
  so   lock hearts
  lock worlds
  and
     and
       and
  our lips we

ALL THE TREE'S HANDS

All the tree's hands
hung empty
               of dark and rain

and we stood beneath them
breathing twilight as a smoke
never touching
                  nor looking anywhere but up.

We cried for those high hung hands
to touch us, a blessing or laying on of,
some touch we had not owned.
                        The hands
hung high and empty of us, making no sign
or gesture,
               leaving us to love
and that gentleness
                  after
                     among trees.

WASHING

Madras
bleeds
in the water

in Madras
unblessed
women

bleed.
My wash water
turns red

my body
begins one
of a thousand

journeys.

LIMES

I will forget the child. There is
a bowl of limes in the refrigerator.
Cool. Sharp.
         At heart bitter, rind
the color of pain.

This morning it rains. Straight down
like hair. Too dark to be morning.
                By afternoon
I have forgotten, put lime in the gin
and afternoon is bright as the morning
should have been.
         The pain, low down, survives
as the child won't, the thought and image whole.

         Rain improves
the twilight bringing down a proper dark
and in the refrigerator the last of the limes,
cool as death, casts its pale green shadow
on the cheek of a white bowl,
                and the soul
of the child, like a pale green lizard
under leaves, flickers away
unseen.

CYCLE

Inside
      a small itch, drop
of blood running
              out, child's life
running out. It's called cunt
and it's that
         and this child's door.
More than that
           is gift, gift gotten,
sweet crease of the girl,
               lips to the man.
And even that over,
covered,
        poor old pompadour
knows
      inside,
         like a drop of blood running,
            a small itch.

STICK FIGURES

At home we'd
draw spindly sidewalk men and women
with their arms out, small
big-headed children to make our own
and grown-up incredibly beautiful
images of ourselves.
                              Now
it is easier to write letters
than talk to you,
the sharp edges of your eyes
like lumps of coal
write messages at my feet.
This way
where your eyes are in my mind
on this paper
I write my name
twice
as if you look at me.

And I look at you through these words
and find I've drawn the same old stick figures
in which there is no beauty
merely truth: your hand
in mine
                   and one small smudged figure walking away.

IT IS TIME

Again
I have come out of your words
as out of my own dying,
premises lying in my hands like cabbage roses.

Believing what was
was real, what wasn't
was dead fruit
I eat what I can.

Lamplight, love's sister,
lived beside our bed
and kept us.
        Darkness is what
my hands hold now, my old lightbulb
                blown out.

It is time and your words
ring for me
        for my body's stone clapper

an echo no longer young
runs ahead of its own death.

GESTURE

I

The rose
lies down
on the grave.

At the widow's back
a wind rises
in which
there are roses,

plays with her
clothes in his
old way.

II

Forgive the rose
its native gesture,
forgive it love
and opening,
and darkened
forgive it
death.

III

In front of her
the wind is
going home.

In back of her
the rose
lies down
brilliant beneath
a silt of rain.

WIDOW MENDING

I

It started
when you left.
Everything enlarged.
My bed
a barge
in an echo chamber.
Night a wind
blowing to Canada and past.
That ceiling a table
to eat from.
Lamplight
hollow, diffuse
as sand. I walked carpets
like deserts of my mind.

II

The first night
your body came out of the dream's distance
toward our old archway
was the first time I smiled.
You were the right size
and the world scaled down again.
How glad I was you came holding
the flame of my life in your hand.

III

How your words inhabit me
now that my rooms eat their own perspective.
I wonder sometimes if I live
where you live
under the ground
but most times walking around
I touch the answer with my tongue.

IV

You know
I forget how to kiss, can not now
somehow conceive of that act
as if it were a grace I've always lacked.
But the fact is it's all right
at least for now, now that everything's
the right size, now that conversation
is become natural to us, now that
to be alive is all right
though it's something else than it was
and there are graces to recover
like kissing, like someone
to love me.

NOT QUICK ENOUGH

Oh I do not remember:

coins in the air drop
stroke by stroke
sound like a clock

all that money

time costing
what it costs
an invention dearer than even itself.

Stealth moves in me
as I turn
like a tuning fork
remembering

how you moved
from dark to light and back
in summer and heat

yet I do not
remember all of it

all time's money spent

and the clock
counting coins
on hot summer nights

when you were here
inventing the dark

and I was
not quick enough
to hold it, to remember it.

I CAN'T HEAR YOU

What are you saying?
What you meant
is gone
and what we knew then
we don't know now.
                        We meant
to save everything but everything
began to wear out.
                        We threw away
first things, found others, you found me.

You were my first
                        shining in your first
of many ages. And you came in me
each time as a first.
                        Not to have been
with anyone else
                        was what you meant.
What are you saying?
                        I can't hear you, your
first dying, the wish I meant to give,
I can't hear any of it now
as if
        you never meant me to.

NOT WHAT

you leave
on my skin

after love

nor in
my hair

will I take
like winding
clothes
to my death

but the bearing:

a head well set,
easy hands,
and eyelids
closed on

all
you made
me.

WIDOW AT NIGHT

This the long night shall foreclose
arms spread angel-fashion toward a moist dream
thighs spread to old angles
and sheet tangles holding down what heaves.
Loneliness to turn to as pillow as moonlight spread
across the bed shining as the man once did there
when the lone woman was half fit to half
and whole in the dark as not now all of a part.
This body in sleep spread to hope, in dream
spread, in dark open as a melon all seeded and
need innocent on her face as life makes
her innocent of it, as the gone man
who loved her, of her fast held love spreading
its need only as sleep lays her open
and night forecloses
what it owns.

CHILD'S POCKET

It is not easy
to move from the first sorrow
toward the next. There are habits
none would cultivate.
                    Taking that first sorrow on
like clothes, dressing for the next
and not allowing for joy
is like lying down
with all the shining young men

and finding the crease of your sex
sewn up like a child's pocket
against loss
                    and against any
possibility of wealth.

PHOTOGRAPHS

Not
that time stopped then
or your beauty held itself tight
as the going back

but
a face
from its time to this–
I mean
love lived then
that steals my laughter now.

You
don't get any older,
one hair a day
my head turns white
and I'm not quite the same.
My face looks out of its last metaphor
into its first.

Not
that I'd wind time back
on its used spindle toward
those washed hours of our arrivals
but holding your lustless beauty thus
I trust the facts of my life less,
the dedications more.

SECOND LOVE

I search, love, and you
are everywhere

my body is all endings

and you look up
from a glass of cool water

touch my cheek
as a blowing leaf

fill my hands
as the silk of my clothes

my body questions and begins

your spoken words read
from the walls

your promises your wishes
my past brim as liquid

I search, love,
with you everywhere

like a future.